Meet You In The Soup

Written By **Cheryl E. Hill**
Illustrated By **Della Burns**

Copyright © 2003 Cheryl E. Hill
United States of America
ISBN-13: 978-0-9859770-1-6
ISBN-10: 0985977019

Preface

Many years have passed since my childhood.

My life was simple, but rich with love.

Warm feelings bubble inside remembering my happiness.

Meet you in the Soup is about my memories as a little girl.
Remembering times spent with my grandma, Ma-Ma, lulls me into a safe space.
Growing up in the old colored Greenline neighborhood of Greenville, South Carolina in the late 1940's to early 1950's; although long ago;
but, yet, seems like only yesterday.

Growing up in these times was not a time deemed as celebratory equality for African American citizens in the story of our history in
the United States of America. But all the while, I was happy in the charmed innocence of childhood and loved living in
Ma-Ma's house; wrapped in a protective cocoon of love away from any and all Boogie Men in a child's imagination. Ma-Ma's house was a
Shot-gun house with rooms straight through.

It was so much love in that house. It was a mansion to me.
And, love makes all the difference, no matter what the times may have been.

The favorite good-bye parting words between my grandma and me

in the mornings as Ma-Ma left for work
were the loving words; "Meet You in the Soup,"
meaning, good-bye, for now, in this morning time,
until we meet again at day's end, in time for family dinner and soup!

Dedication

To: Ma-Ma, my grandma, Mrs. Grace Elizabeth Thomas Gordon
Ma-Ma lived a long, happy life.
October 10, 1912-June 18, 2009

To: My mother, Marian Gordon Montgomery, my grandma's only child,
a beloved princess; and, as the granddaughter,
I basked in the royal magic dust of love
sprinkling down upon me.

"Wake up sleepy head," cajoled Ma-Ma.
I smiled inside with happiness.
The sound of Ma-Ma's voice and the nearness of her made me feel warm and loved.
Her nearness made me feel safe, too.

Half dreaming still, I remembered the night before.
I'd awakened frightened by the darkness of the house.
Ma-Ma came to my rescue as usual.

She gave me hot milk with vanilla added.
It soothed me to sleep again.

Then just before dawn, before the rooster crowed
cockle doodle doo,
as it always happened, I had to go potty.
If I had to do number one,
I used the big chamber pot next to Ma-Ma's bed.

But if I had to do number two,
I used the bathroom on the back porch.
I was never afraid with my Ma-Ma standing by.

Good yummy smells from the kitchen tickled my nose,
and awakened me gently from my sleeping dreams.

"Come on child! Hurry! Wash your face and hands so you can eat!"
Ma-Ma handed me a warm, soapy washcloth.

Ma-Ma stood by watching me clean my facc and hands.
"Come on! Be quick! Your grits are waiting!
Don't want them to get cold!"
Ma-Ma urged hurriedly, as she sashshayed from the room.

Trailing after Ma-Ma, straight through to the kitchen I went.

There on the kitchen table was a bowl of hot, steamy grits with creamy butter and chunks of New York Sharp cheese melting on top! I dug eagerly into my favorite food of all; grits and cheese. Um-um, what a treat!

While I ate, Ma-Ma hustled and bustled about like a streak of lightening! She dusted and cleaned, here, there, and everywhere!

Ma-Ma was a domestic worker she cleaned other ladies' houses.
But, she always hurried to clean her own house before going off to theirs.

It was amazing how fast Ma-Ma could work.
She seemed to have more hands than most people.
She could so many things all at once!

When Ma-Ma was finally content with her house,
she would speed straight ahead to get ready to leave for work.
I followed reluctantly behind her.

I followed Ma-Ma to the front porch.
We hugged and kissed.
I whispered our loving, good-bye words to her.
"Meet you in the soup," Ma-Ma.
"Meet you in the soup, Checky," Ma-Ma whispered, cooingly,
back to me.

I stood on the front porch watching Ma-Ma
as far as I could see her.
Before turning the corner to be lost from my eyesight, Ma-Ma turned once
more to look back at me. Blowing me a kiss, she shouted,
"Meet you in the soup, Checky!"

I stood on my tiptoes.
I raised myself to be as tall as I could be.
Cupping my hands around my mouth, I bellowed from the top of my lungs:
"Meet you in the soup, Ma-Ma!"

About the Author

Cheryl Elizabeth Hill graduate from D. C. Teachers College (now the University of the District of Columbia) with a B.S, In Elementary Education. She received her M.A. from the University of Texas at San Antonio. Mrs. Hill began teaching at age 22; and, taught in public schools for forty years. Mrs. Hill resides in the Greater Houston Area with her husband, three adult children, and grandchildren. Greenville, South Carolina is Mrs. Hill's native home; it is the setting of her book: *Meet You in the Soup.*

www.ingramcontent.com/pod-product-compliance
Lightning Source LLC
LaVergne TN
LVHW071031070426
835507LV00002B/112